Write or Die

~ My Solace in The Wilderness~

By: Shameeka Williams

Copyright © 2016
Shameeka Williams
All rights reserved
ISBN:061586001X
ISBN 13:978-0615860015

~Don't let the Wilderness eat you alive

make them wait until you die~

~Contents~

Welcome to the wilderness

1. Alone/ Ambition

2. Burning-Buildings/Betrayal/Blood Stains

3. Collateral damage

4. Death

5. Emancipated

6. Forgiveness/ False Prophets

7. Greed

8. Heartless

9. Injustice

10. Jealousy

11. Kindness

12. Loyalty

13. Motherless/Motherhood/Misconceptions

14. Naked
15. Opportunity
16. Predators
17. Respect
18. Solace
19. Truth/Trust Issues
20. Ulterior Motives
21. Vulnerability
22. Watered Gardens
23. Your Wilderness

Welcome to the Wilderness

The Wilderness will eat you whole
if you allow it
The Beasts will sip
envy, jealousy and betrayal
Then come for you in the night
To Devour your energy
You must protect it at all cost
Find your Shield
Find Your Solace
Or face your demise
They will feed you plenty
False emotions and lies
They will steal your joy
With their protruding Pride
They will come as sheep
But really wolves inside
Your sanity is their entrée
And they are known to clean plates
Bellies filled with spirits

They sucked out along the way
Then we wonder why they have many faces
The lies of the night
Reveal in the day
Shit gets real in the wilderness
Battered beast still behave
Afraid to see beyond the wilderness
Mentally a happy slave
Freedom is hidden well
In the wilderness
You must be willing to seek
Your truth is in the wilderness
You must be willing to speak

Alone in the Wilderness

I felt alone in the wilderness once
Tears fell like leaves daily
My heart ached from pain
Unapologetic actions
Caused an Assassination
 of my love and dedication
Character destroyed
To save yours
I still held on
Hoping that one day
We would walk away
 from the wilderness
Find a safe place
To call our own
Raise our babies
To have Pride, Respect and
A mind that's strong
I'm finding my way
out of the wilderness
And one day I'll be free

Until then I find peace
 in the wilderness
Until peace finds me

Ambition in the Wilderness

Ambition comes at a price
in the wilderness
You must be willing to pay
Or the Beasts will use
 your hunger against you
They'll dangle opportunity
 in your face
Only to snatch it away
At first sight of greatness
And because you possess
the potential to be
greater than them
You are now considered
 a threat
So, they gather and plan
 your demise
The whole time feeding you lies
Like "I got you"
Or "you got what it takes"
If you're smart

you'll play your part
And realize they're snakes
So, keep a close eye
For your fate's sake
Don't be so quick
to trust a beast
That likes to "save face"
They'll be quick to
 throw your soul
On their flamed stakes

Burning Buildings in the Wilderness

It danced around her
thirsty for her flesh
hoping no one would claim her
being too consumed by fear
the burning building wanted
her innocence
intoxicated by her tears
Burning bodies in
the burning buildings
The secrets don't go away
They'll dance around
the burning bodies
On the fire escape
The beasts appear
once the smoke clears
Hoping no one saw a thing
But guilt lies beneath
And you'll reap
Your burning flame

Betrayal in the Wilderness

You never see it coming
It creeps up like a
 thief in the night
The stench of betrayal
is like none other
It adheres to the
 souls of the weak
The beasts eat
 everything in sight
Under the moonlight
Betrayal looks like
the prettiest rose
you've ever seen
If it sticks around
until the daylight
You'll see the
 truth revealed
through every beam
some actions
can be forgiven

those that
cannot create
a thirst
the only way
to quench it
is revenge
the hatred
sinks in
there's no
coming back
from cruel things
that have happened

Blood Stains in the Wilderness

Run me a bath, Mother
Some stains are harder
to remove than others
I've been visiting
with grandmother
She taught me
how to protect myself
The lesson was a little messy
I believe I wet myself
Please don't ask me anymore, mother
I like to forget those stains
His blood was on my face and clothes
And I don't even know his name
Please don't wash my laundry, mother
I never want to wear those clothes again
Blood stains in the wilderness
Don't wash away
It doesn't matter
If you're a sinner
Or a saint

Collateral damage in the Wilderness

Some beasts never intend
 to hurt their young
And protect them at all costs
But what about
the damaged beasts
Who know only pain
All innocent in the path
 of the damaged beast
Will be sacrificed
For there is no honor
amongst beasts
In the wilderness
Every day survived
is a day to thrive
Or you'll be eating alive
or left to die
 sometimes death is
 the only healing
The damaged can receive
There's no remorse

from the beasts
They see no wrong
in how they feast
As long as they eat

Death in the Wilderness

I died a thousand times that night
Didn't cause any grief for the beasts
They carried on as if my death
Was long overdue
Delighted that I no longer
walked the earth
They laughed, filled their bellies
Enjoyed my absence
A little more than I expected
My soul watched in disbelief
Disrespected by those I held so dear
I'm almost glad I'm no longer here
Pain will never touch me again
No beast will pretend to love me
Then hurt me again
I died a thousand times that night
Didn't cause any grief for the beast
He didn't shed any tears
Didn't lose any sleep
In that moment

I realized
You are who you keep

Emancipated in the Wilderness

The moment I've longed for
Is finally here
So why am I so unsure
Is it because when I wanted to hear yes
They were dead set on saying no
And now that freedom
Is fast approaching
I'm afraid to let go
Afraid that once I'm grown
They won't love me no more
Because just as I have been longing to be free
They have been longing to be free of me
Free from providing basic needs
Free from responsibility
Emancipated profoundly at 15
The hands were washed
The locks were changed
Their backs were turned
Nothing was the same

Forgiveness in the Wilderness

The art of forgiveness
Is simply one day at a time
But you first must understand
Who, what and why
you are forgiving
Or not so forgiving
It will not happen over night
Nor will it be a smooth walk
Through the wilderness
The beasts will see
no wrongs in their actions
They will force you to sip
 from the cup of confusion
And feast on guilt
Hoping to force you into forgiveness
To save them the trip
Those guilty travels
Are hard to forget

False Prophets in the Wilderness

We're supposed to Honor them
For they
Can do
No wrong
But how
Can one
Exhibit honor
When evil
Is so
Strong
Often wrapped
In blood
Opposite
Of how
They carry-on
Water is preferred
Early on
Family portraits
Torn
A child scorned

Too busy
To provide
Shelter
During the storm
Yet they demand
Loyalty
Don't you dare
Deprive empathy
For they will
Show no
Sympathy
When they
Erase your History

Greed in the Wilderness

It's not enough that you control my life
You want to control my mind too
Program me to do as you say
But not as you do
If I was you I would only want one of me too
Because greed shouldn't come in pairs
Only love should come in two's
You feel entitled to everything that doesn't
Belong to you
And take credit for everything that
You put no effort to
You want more than you deserve
Yet give so less
You suck the soul out of
Anyone on the pursuit of happiness

Heartless in the Wilderness

You question her actions
As if unaware to the things
That made her so cold
Lines were crossed
Lies were told
Predators preyed on precious souls
But you're more concerned
As to why she's cold
Heartless to the bullshit
And constant no shows
She felt it was best to let go
No need to tend to wounds any further
The beast take secrets to their grave
So, there's no record how they've misbehave
Yet you are threatened by her cold shoulder
Did you think the ice would melt away?
As she got older
Maybe forget the things you displayed
When you disowned her
Front porches don't seem too nice

When doors are closed on ya
When emails go unanswered
And calls go directly to voicemail
Do you sit there and "oh Well"?
Or take time to reflect
Like when was the last time
I showed her respect
When was the first time
I said some shit I shouldn't have said
How many times did I let those likes
Go to my head
But you wonder why she's incapable
Of giving a fuck
For the first time in forever she realizes
She wasted too much
TIME
In a room with where egos
Just consume too much
And the ears that hear the pain
Truly give no fucks
If it's not gossip, drama or bullshit
They don't drink from positive cups
That much

Life choices are much different
Solely connected to be nosey
Not to keep it touch
And it's only when they want
 or wanna know Something
That they say what's up
But her being heartless
Bothers you
Oh, how the things that should
truly matter
Doesn't stick like glue
The pot will call the kettle black
A thousand times
Before the kettles yells
"look at you"
And even in that moment
The pot still won't follow suit
It will overlook every one of its flaws
Because the lie it lives
Is better than its ugly truth

Injustice in the Wilderness

It starts with a J
And ends with an E
Unbeknown to you and me
Something we have yet to see
Deprived since the days of slavery
Yet here we are in 2016
Still waiting for our
Black lives to matter
247 365
Not just when it's all-star weekend
Or super bowl night
Still waiting on the bullets
To stop
The accountability to start
Still waiting on the Justice system
To play its part

Jealousy in the Wilderness

You should never trust a beast
Most certainly not a jealous one
They'll steal your joy in the moonlight
Wear your pain to reflect the sun
Those jealous beasts
Are truly tricky ones
Overly competitive
When they don't have to be
Instead of perfecting relationships
They rather belittle the weak
Their strength comes without dignity
They feast on impurities
 You should never trust a jealous beast
There's no telling
What lies beneath
What brings them joy
What brings them grief
What soothes their soul
What helps them sleep
One must wonder if

They enjoy
The company
They keep
Or do they
Role play well
Amongst the sheep
Of course, the sheep
Don't notice
They're always
Fucking sleep
But those cut
From a different
Cloth
Always seem
To peep.

Kindness in the Wilderness

When from the heart
It can be a beautiful thing
Ever taken for granted
Sometimes will leave a sting
Be cautious with your kindness
But don't be stingy
There is a difference
Beast take kindness for weakness
Without a second thought
They will rob you blind
With a smile on their face
Because you're blinded by kindness
They hope to never get caught
Guilt doesn't come for them
They sleep peaceful
with their stolen goods
they laugh at the thought
of prosecution
if the dead could talk
one must hope like hell

they would
even the voice of the wronged
couldn't force them to do good

Loyalty in the Wilderness

For some it is a gift and a curse
The gift of loyalty
is like none other
it's deeper than
what a child feels for its mother
Loyalty has been known
To ruin
Which presents the curse
Loyalty should be priceless
But for the right price
Some will lose sight
And take flight
Never looking back
Leaving one to question
How could another do
something like that
But never once question
 your own actions
Blinded by bloodlines
Did you ever take time

To understand how valuable
Your loyalty is
It's not safe to give it
to everyone
That comes your way
You'll may never know
How much they'll take
To seal your fate

Motherless in the Wilderness

Forced to walk alone in a world so cold
Tormented by reckless souls
At what age
Do you stop needing, wanting or loving
Your mother?
I pray I live long enough to see that age
Rather than pour my pain
On this fucking page
Pardon my rage
But I was 19
Viewed as grown
Because I had a seed
Do you know how many nights
My grown ass
Wanted my mommy!!!!!!
Pray for me
Pray that the days get easier
And the good memories
Don't fade
I was 19

Motherless in a wilderness
That never did shit for me
It damaged my beautiful queen
And her absence damaged me
Much deeper than the present
Mental illness is an ugly beast
Shatters bonds
To say the least
Broken promises, homes and souls
Motherless in a wilderness
So cold

Motherhood in the Wilderness

I gave life in the wilderness once
The greatest gift bestowed on me
By the most high
Even though young in age
Becoming a mother
Saved my life
I walked a path of destruction
Unbothered and not afraid
He calmed my wild spirit
On the 19th day of May

I raised my child in the wilderness
Made many mistakes
Along the way
If I could erase any pain
I've caused
I would
And hope like hell
that he would be ok
Actions of others

would have no
influence on him
His path is his to walk
Yet I'm protective of him

Misconceptions in the Wilderness

There is often a misconception in the wilderness
That the beasts will be gentle and kind
Because you have been gentle and kind to them
Don't be fooled
Always do unto others
As they do unto you
You cannot force beasts to be kind
You cannot force them to own
All their flaws
Much less not worry about yours
So, you could love a beast
A thousand times
And the one time
You need that beast to love you back
They will fall short
Caught up in the moment
Of distraction
Irrelevant conversations

Providing limited satisfaction
There is often a misconception
In the wilderness
That if you love the beast
It will love you back
It's not in his nature
To provide that

Naked in the Wilderness

Many moons ago I bared my soul
Beneath the stars
Before a beast unlike no other
Bloodied drunk with lust
Our bodies connected on a level
No other beast could understand
Could he look beyond my beauty
And accept my inner beast?
Did I look into the eyes of a beast and see
Love hidden deep and hidden well
I became his right
He became my wrong
We created the greatest
Love spell
No matter how far thee
Goes
Thou know that home is home
And if allowed to roam
It will not last longer than a full moon

Have you ever been naked
In the wilderness
Took time to let someone in
Share a piece of yourself
You keep buried within

Opportunity in the Wilderness

If the moment to be better than
you were the day before
arrived on your doorstep
would you answer the door?
Or hide away
Because you are not ready for change
And the thought of being a better person
Makes you feel strange
yet the thought of being fucked up
keeps you still
wanting nothing more
for someone to keep it real
never acquiring any life skills
the art of ignorance
is so real
wanting more in your environment
sometimes gets you killed
because you wanted the opportunity
to be great
you wanted the opportunity

to be equal
you wanted the opportunity
to be respected
but opportunity
doesn't knock twice
if it ever knocks at all

Predators in the Wilderness

Some prefer to prey on the weak
Only at night
Others commit their acts
In plain sight
It sends a rush
During daylight
Remorse is scarce
There is no wrong or right
The scent of the innocent
Is unbearable for the beast
He enjoys the fact
His prey is too young
To speak
And while it's mother
Is fast asleep
The beast creeps

I fell asleep in the wilderness once
Rudely awakened by a wild beast
He devoured my energy
And enslaved me mentally
I couldn't tell a soul
What he did to me
Because I wasn't sure if it was wrong
Or if it was meant for me
Planted a seed that didn't get to flourish
So, deep in fear I almost gave him something so gorgeous
More than my soul
But he'd never notice
I let go............

Have you ever danced with a beast at noon?
Only to hide from him at midnight
That was my day
That was my night
That was my nightmare
That was my life
He used to call himself Mr. right
I beg to differ
Because a Mr.
Would treat his Mrs.
Right
Protect her and uplift her
Not strip her of Rights
The Right to be Free
The Right to be Me
The Right to show my face to my family
Without the whispers and stares
Elephant shit Everywhere!!!!!
Because the animal
has yet to be addressed
Not sure whom to ask for help
In my pursuit of happiness
I know for a fact this isn't it

I used to hang out and vibe with my friends
Now I'm dodging punches and kicks
 Took the warning and I kept moving
 it was easier back then just to cut the cord and keep it moving.
Could somebody tell me
Exactly what the fuck
I'm doing
Because I've lost so much
Now everything is fucking ruined
And I can't undo what was done to me
Or in front of me
So far from recovery

Respect in the Wilderness

It's rarely giving
Much better when earned
Provided to the wrong one
It could leave your soul burned
Never questioned
When mutually applied
Bonds are created
Trust coincides
Your circle is filled
With ride or dies
But don't be blind
Sometimes it collides
With its rival
Pride
Jumped by envy
Poisoned by jealousy
If you don't have respect
For yourself
How the fuck do I
Expect you to have

Respect for me
Let's not revisit
Loyalty
You notice everything
Except for what
You've done to me

Solace in the Wilderness

Until the flesh of those
Who have wronged, robbed or preyed
Is rested in a shallow grave
I will find solace
In the simple things
Lemonade and chicken wings
Pardon me
This load is normally
Heavy
But right now
I have
Light feet
How do I deal
With this shit
I find solace
In the weirdest Shit
I remember
How the scabs
Use to heal up
Quick

*Not every scar
is visible
not every promise
is legit
these things
will cause pain
in the wilderness
unless you find
solace in it
don't go insane
in the wilderness
trying to make sense
of all
live in the moment
in the wilderness
and you'll conquer
it all*

Truth in the Wilderness

Some say what's done in the dark
Gets revealed in the light
But some truths shine brighter in moonlight
Because the sun doesn't appreciate
What's in plain sight
Many truths are revealed
During the night life
It's easier that way
Too much judgement
During the day
After midnight
Everyone's demons come
Out to play
The fearful sleep
The fearless eat
You'll understand once
You hear the belly speak
To be strong is to survive
For others, it means to devour the meek
Most don't grasp in time

And become counted sheep.
The wilderness is no place
For the weak

I revealed truth in the wilderness once
Sleepless nights filled my heart with regret
I refused to have those stains
Imprinted on the heart
Of one I love, so dear
I opened the door
Without fear
Worried not of what
Some would say
Worried more about
Clearing my conscious
And creating a way
For a bond that should
Have been solid
To take its place
On the right path
Instead barricades were formed
Barb wires covered in jealousy
Should I have complied
After they directed me
Or resisted
And demanded that
They respected me

Allowed me
To share my truth
Maybe love
Could have
Survived
But they
Never let it be

Trust issues in the Wilderness

They arrive at your doorstep
Carrying a luggage of lies
Making the visit
More impersonal
Than they realize
Oh, how I
Despise
The forced hugs
And guilty eyes
So, my distance
Should come as
No surprise
Yet you question it
Repeated actions
Causes trust to die
Love soon follows
Then respect
Subsides
Sides are chosen
Lies are told

And prides collide
How can you trust
Someone that
Has too much pride
To admit
They fucked up
And I don't mean
Partied too much
I mean gave themselves
To another
Or violated the laws
Of being a mother
Or simply fell short
Or loving another
So, pardon
My selfishness
My trust
Isn't for everybody
I'm a selfish Bitch
So, I've been told
But those beasts didn't
Know the half of it
If you have a minute

I'll help you understand
Some shit
The first time
I faced a liar
It was at the age
Of 6
He had hand
Problems
His hands
Truly loved
The kids
I have removed
More knives
Then I
Can count
Placed by
Those
I never knew
Were enemies
Once understood
Nothing is guaranteed
Not blood
marriage

*Or planted seeds
So, I had a few
Moments
Of clarity
Watered
my own
garden
and removed
those
damaged seeds
trust issues
created
a damaged beast*

Ulterior Motives in the Wilderness

Some gifts come from within
Some have shackles attached
Invisible to the naked eye
They'll hang on to that
So, when the time
Presents itself
The art of giving
Will mean nothing
Because the only
Reason you received
Those gifts
Were because
The giver
Wanted something
And that
Something
Will remain
Unknown
Until they
Are through

With fronting
Motives revealed
The gates of truth
Have been opened
Next time
Use caution

Vulnerability in the Wilderness

Temptation devours the weak
Without remorse
And in an instant
Everything is lost
Who's to blame
For actions
Completed
while weak
the serpent
that slithered
or the
raging beast
who responded
in accordance
to any other beast
the jezebels
capture souls
quietly
while they sleep

Watered gardens in the Wilderness

Oh, how beauty
Blossoms
In watered gardens
Flaws are soon
Forgotten
Strength is restored
And faith
Is locked in
Trust grows
As the wind
Blows
Watered gardens
Are beautiful
It's incredible
The power
that
Nature holds
Closely studied
Never controlled

Your Wilderness

Filled with everything

Designed to break you

From the moment

You arrive

Your life

Is in shackles

It is up

To you

To escape

Is it up

To you

To be

Great

It is up to you

To separate

The real from

The fake

Your wilderness

Is your own

To Conquer

No one else
Can assist
That's how
Problems
Are created
Taking on
Extra shit
You know
What can
Can't
And won't be
You know
Your breaking point
It's not up
To me
You know
You're not
Making sense
Yet
You brain pick me
what I digest
Doesn't help
You shit

Your wilderness
And my wilderness
Doesn't consist
Of the same
Shit
The things you accept
May push me away
You couldn't
Handle
The wilderness
I've endured
You're not
Built that way
Your wilderness
Is your own
To live
Learn
And find
Your own
Solace
If you demand respect
and steer clear of false prophets
you'll escape your wilderness

believe in yourself
you got this!!!!!!

To learn more about the Author
You may visit her websites and social media
Twitter: @INDIE_BK_JEWEL
Facebook: HAPPY2BEINDIEJEWEL
indiejewelshameekawilliams.weebly.com

www.ingramcontent.com/pod-product-compliance
Lightning Source LLC
Chambersburg PA
CBHW022124040426
42450CB00006B/842